WEBSITE ADDRESS BOOK

SITE NAME:

SITE ADDRESS:

USERNAME:

PASSWORD:

NOTE:

SITE NAME:

SITE ADDRESS:

USERNAME:

PASSWORD:

NOTE:

SITE NAME:

SITE ADDRESS:

USERNAME:

PASSWORD:

NOTE:

SITE NAME:

SITE ADDRESS:

USERNAME:

PASSWORD:

NOTE:

SITE NAME:

SITE ADDRESS:

USERNAME:

PASSWORD:

NOTE:

SITE NAME:

SITE ADDRESS:

USERNAME:

PASSWORD:

NOTE:

SITE NAME:

SITE ADDRESS:

USERNAME:

PASSWORD:

NOTE:

SITE NAME:

SITE ADDRESS:

USERNAME:

PASSWORD:

NOTE:

SITE NAME:

SITE ADDRESS:

USERNAME:

PASSWORD:

NOTE:

SITE NAME:

SITE ADDRESS:

USERNAME:

PASSWORD:

NOTE:

SITE NAME:

SITE ADDRESS:

USERNAME:

PASSWORD:

NOTE:

SITE NAME:

SITE ADDRESS:

USERNAME:

PASSWORD:

NOTE:

SITE NAME:

SITE ADDRESS:

USERNAME:

PASSWORD:

NOTE:

SITE NAME:

SITE ADDRESS:

USERNAME:

PASSWORD:

NOTE:

SITE NAME:

SITE ADDRESS:

USERNAME:

PASSWORD:

NOTE:

SITE NAME:

SITE ADDRESS:

USERNAME:

PASSWORD:

NOTE:

SITE NAME:

SITE ADDRESS:

USERNAME:

PASSWORD:

NOTE:

SITE NAME:

SITE ADDRESS:

USERNAME:

PASSWORD:

NOTE:

SITE NAME:

SITE ADDRESS:

USERNAME:

PASSWORD:

NOTE:

SITE NAME:

SITE ADDRESS:

USERNAME:

PASSWORD:

NOTE:

SITE NAME:

SITE ADDRESS:

USERNAME:

PASSWORD:

NOTE:

SITE NAME:

SITE ADDRESS:

USERNAME:

PASSWORD:

NOTE:

SITE NAME:

SITE ADDRESS:

USERNAME:

PASSWORD:

NOTE:

SITE NAME:

SITE ADDRESS:

USERNAME:

PASSWORD:

NOTE:

SITE NAME:

SITE ADDRESS:

USERNAME:

PASSWORD:

NOTE:

SITE NAME:

SITE ADDRESS:

USERNAME:

PASSWORD:

NOTE:

SITE NAME:

SITE ADDRESS:

USERNAME:

PASSWORD:

NOTE:

SITE NAME:

SITE ADDRESS:

USERNAME:

PASSWORD:

NOTE:

SITE NAME:

SITE ADDRESS:

USERNAME:

PASSWORD:

NOTE:

SITE NAME:

SITE ADDRESS:

USERNAME:

PASSWORD:

NOTE:

SITE NAME:

SITE ADDRESS:

USERNAME:

PASSWORD:

NOTE:

SITE NAME:

SITE ADDRESS:

USERNAME:

PASSWORD:

NOTE:

SITE NAME:

SITE ADDRESS:

USERNAME:

PASSWORD:

NOTE:

SITE NAME:

SITE ADDRESS:

USERNAME:

PASSWORD:

NOTE:

SITE NAME:

SITE ADDRESS:

USERNAME:

PASSWORD:

NOTE:

SITE NAME:

SITE ADDRESS:

USERNAME:

PASSWORD:

NOTE:

SITE NAME:

SITE ADDRESS:

USERNAME:

PASSWORD:

NOTE:

SITE NAME:

SITE ADDRESS:

USERNAME:

PASSWORD:

NOTE:

SITE NAME:

SITE ADDRESS:

USERNAME:

PASSWORD:

NOTE:

SITE NAME:

SITE ADDRESS:

USERNAME:

PASSWORD:

NOTE:

SITE NAME:

SITE ADDRESS:

USERNAME:

PASSWORD:

NOTE:

SITE NAME:

SITE ADDRESS:

USERNAME:

PASSWORD:

NOTE:

SITE NAME:

SITE ADDRESS:

USERNAME:

PASSWORD:

NOTE:

SITE NAME:

SITE ADDRESS:

USERNAME:

PASSWORD:

NOTE:

SITE NAME:

SITE ADDRESS:

USERNAME:

PASSWORD:

NOTE:

SITE NAME:

SITE ADDRESS:

USERNAME:

PASSWORD:

NOTE:

SITE NAME:

SITE ADDRESS:

USERNAME:

PASSWORD:

NOTE:

SITE NAME:

SITE ADDRESS:

USERNAME:

PASSWORD:

NOTE:

SITE NAME:

SITE ADDRESS:

USERNAME:

PASSWORD:

NOTE:

SITE NAME:

SITE ADDRESS:

USERNAME:

PASSWORD:

NOTE:

SITE NAME:

SITE ADDRESS:

USERNAME:

PASSWORD:

NOTE:

SITE NAME:

SITE ADDRESS:

USERNAME:

PASSWORD:

NOTE:

SITE NAME:

SITE ADDRESS:

USERNAME:

PASSWORD:

NOTE:

SITE NAME:

SITE ADDRESS:

USERNAME:

PASSWORD:

NOTE:

SITE NAME:

SITE ADDRESS:

USERNAME:

PASSWORD:

NOTE:

SITE NAME:

SITE ADDRESS:

USERNAME:

PASSWORD:

NOTE:

SITE NAME:

SITE ADDRESS:

USERNAME:

PASSWORD:

NOTE:

SITE NAME:

SITE ADDRESS:

USERNAME:

PASSWORD:

NOTE:

SITE NAME:

SITE ADDRESS:

USERNAME:

PASSWORD:

NOTE:

SITE NAME:

SITE ADDRESS:

USERNAME:

PASSWORD:

NOTE:

SITE NAME:

SITE ADDRESS:

USERNAME:

PASSWORD:

NOTE:

SITE NAME:

SITE ADDRESS:

USERNAME:

PASSWORD:

NOTE:

SITE NAME:

SITE ADDRESS:

USERNAME:

PASSWORD:

NOTE:

SITE NAME:

SITE ADDRESS:

USERNAME:

PASSWORD:

NOTE:

SITE NAME:

SITE ADDRESS:

USERNAME:

PASSWORD:

NOTE:

SITE NAME:

SITE ADDRESS:

USERNAME:

PASSWORD:

NOTE:

SITE NAME:

SITE ADDRESS:

USERNAME:

PASSWORD:

NOTE:

SITE NAME:

SITE ADDRESS:

USERNAME:

PASSWORD:

NOTE:

SITE NAME:

SITE ADDRESS:

USERNAME:

PASSWORD:

NOTE:

SITE NAME:

SITE ADDRESS:

USERNAME:

PASSWORD:

NOTE:

SITE NAME:

SITE ADDRESS:

USERNAME:

PASSWORD:

NOTE:

SITE NAME:

SITE ADDRESS:

USERNAME:

PASSWORD:

NOTE:

SITE NAME:

SITE ADDRESS:

USERNAME:

PASSWORD:

NOTE:

SITE NAME:

SITE ADDRESS:

USERNAME:

PASSWORD:

NOTE:

SITE NAME:

SITE ADDRESS:

USERNAME:

PASSWORD:

NOTE:

SITE NAME:

SITE ADDRESS:

USERNAME:

PASSWORD:

NOTE:

SITE NAME:

SITE ADDRESS:

USERNAME:

PASSWORD:

NOTE:

SITE NAME:

SITE ADDRESS:

USERNAME:

PASSWORD:

NOTE:

SITE NAME:

SITE ADDRESS:

USERNAME:

PASSWORD:

NOTE:

SITE NAME:

SITE ADDRESS:

USERNAME:

PASSWORD:

NOTE:

SITE NAME:

SITE ADDRESS:

USERNAME:

PASSWORD:

NOTE:

SITE NAME:

SITE ADDRESS:

USERNAME:

PASSWORD:

NOTE:

SITE NAME:

SITE ADDRESS:

USERNAME:

PASSWORD:

NOTE:

SITE NAME:

SITE ADDRESS:

USERNAME:

PASSWORD:

NOTE:

SITE NAME:

SITE ADDRESS:

USERNAME:

PASSWORD:

NOTE:

SITE NAME:

SITE ADDRESS:

USERNAME:

PASSWORD:

NOTE:

SITE NAME:

SITE ADDRESS:

USERNAME:

PASSWORD:

NOTE:

SITE NAME:

SITE ADDRESS:

USERNAME:

PASSWORD:

NOTE:

SITE NAME:

SITE ADDRESS:

USERNAME:

PASSWORD:

NOTE:

SITE NAME:

SITE ADDRESS:

USERNAME:

PASSWORD:

NOTE:

SITE NAME:

SITE ADDRESS:

USERNAME:

PASSWORD:

NOTE:

SITE NAME:

SITE ADDRESS:

USERNAME:

PASSWORD:

NOTE:

SITE NAME:

SITE ADDRESS:

USERNAME:

PASSWORD:

NOTE:

SITE NAME:

SITE ADDRESS:

USERNAME:

PASSWORD:

NOTE:

SITE NAME:

SITE ADDRESS:

USERNAME:

PASSWORD:

NOTE:

SITE NAME:

SITE ADDRESS:

USERNAME:

PASSWORD:

NOTE:

SITE NAME:

SITE ADDRESS:

USERNAME:

PASSWORD:

NOTE:

SITE NAME:

SITE ADDRESS:

USERNAME:

PASSWORD:

NOTE:

SITE NAME:

SITE ADDRESS:

USERNAME:

PASSWORD:

NOTE:

SITE NAME:

SITE ADDRESS:

USERNAME:

PASSWORD:

NOTE:

SITE NAME:

SITE ADDRESS:

USERNAME:

PASSWORD:

NOTE:

SITE NAME:

SITE ADDRESS:

USERNAME:

PASSWORD:

NOTE:

SITE NAME:

SITE ADDRESS:

USERNAME:

PASSWORD:

NOTE:

SITE NAME:

SITE ADDRESS:

USERNAME:

PASSWORD:

NOTE:

SITE NAME:

SITE ADDRESS:

USERNAME:

PASSWORD:

NOTE:

SITE NAME:

SITE ADDRESS:

USERNAME:

PASSWORD:

NOTE:

SITE NAME:

SITE ADDRESS:

USERNAME:

PASSWORD:

NOTE:

SITE NAME:

SITE ADDRESS:

USERNAME:

PASSWORD:

NOTE:

SITE NAME:

SITE ADDRESS:

USERNAME:

PASSWORD:

NOTE:

SITE NAME:

SITE ADDRESS:

USERNAME:

PASSWORD:

NOTE:

SITE NAME:

SITE ADDRESS:

USERNAME:

PASSWORD:

NOTE:

SITE NAME:

SITE ADDRESS:

USERNAME:

PASSWORD:

NOTE:

SITE NAME:

SITE ADDRESS:

USERNAME:

PASSWORD:

NOTE:

SITE NAME:

SITE ADDRESS:

USERNAME:

PASSWORD:

NOTE:

SITE NAME:

SITE ADDRESS:

USERNAME:

PASSWORD:

NOTE:

SITE NAME:

SITE ADDRESS:

USERNAME:

PASSWORD:

NOTE:

SITE NAME:

SITE ADDRESS:

USERNAME:

PASSWORD:

NOTE:

SITE NAME:

SITE ADDRESS:

USERNAME:

PASSWORD:

NOTE:

SITE NAME:

SITE ADDRESS:

USERNAME:

PASSWORD:

NOTE:

SITE NAME:

SITE ADDRESS:

USERNAME:

PASSWORD:

NOTE:

SITE NAME:

SITE ADDRESS:

USERNAME:

PASSWORD:

NOTE:

SITE NAME:

SITE ADDRESS:

USERNAME:

PASSWORD:

NOTE:

SITE NAME:

SITE ADDRESS:

USERNAME:

PASSWORD:

NOTE:

SITE NAME:

SITE ADDRESS:

USERNAME:

PASSWORD:

NOTE:

SITE NAME:

SITE ADDRESS:

USERNAME:

PASSWORD:

NOTE:

SITE NAME:

SITE ADDRESS:

USERNAME:

PASSWORD:

NOTE:

SITE NAME:

SITE ADDRESS:

USERNAME:

PASSWORD:

NOTE:

SITE NAME:

SITE ADDRESS:

USERNAME:

PASSWORD:

NOTE:

SITE NAME:

SITE ADDRESS:

USERNAME:

PASSWORD:

NOTE:

SITE NAME:

SITE ADDRESS:

USERNAME:

PASSWORD:

NOTE:

SITE NAME:

SITE ADDRESS:

USERNAME:

PASSWORD:

NOTE:

SITE NAME:

SITE ADDRESS:

USERNAME:

PASSWORD:

NOTE:

SITE NAME:

SITE ADDRESS:

USERNAME:

PASSWORD:

NOTE:

SITE NAME:

SITE ADDRESS:

USERNAME:

PASSWORD:

NOTE:

SITE NAME:

SITE ADDRESS:

USERNAME:

PASSWORD:

NOTE:

SITE NAME:

SITE ADDRESS:

USERNAME:

PASSWORD:

NOTE:

SITE NAME:

SITE ADDRESS:

USERNAME:

PASSWORD:

NOTE:

SITE NAME:

SITE ADDRESS:

USERNAME:

PASSWORD:

NOTE:

SITE NAME:

SITE ADDRESS:

USERNAME:

PASSWORD:

NOTE:

SITE NAME:

SITE ADDRESS:

USERNAME:

PASSWORD:

NOTE:

SITE NAME:

SITE ADDRESS:

USERNAME:

PASSWORD:

NOTE:

SITE NAME:

SITE ADDRESS:

USERNAME:

PASSWORD:

NOTE:

SITE NAME:

SITE ADDRESS:

USERNAME:

PASSWORD:

NOTE:

SITE NAME:

SITE ADDRESS:

USERNAME:

PASSWORD:

NOTE:

SITE NAME:

SITE ADDRESS:

USERNAME:

PASSWORD:

NOTE:

SITE NAME:

SITE ADDRESS:

USERNAME:

PASSWORD:

NOTE:

SITE NAME:

SITE ADDRESS:

USERNAME:

PASSWORD:

NOTE:

SITE NAME:

SITE ADDRESS:

USERNAME:

PASSWORD:

NOTE:

SITE NAME:

SITE ADDRESS:

USERNAME:

PASSWORD:

NOTE:

SITE NAME:

SITE ADDRESS:

USERNAME:

PASSWORD:

NOTE:

SITE NAME:

SITE ADDRESS:

USERNAME:

PASSWORD:

NOTE:

SITE NAME:

SITE ADDRESS:

USERNAME:

PASSWORD:

NOTE:

SITE NAME:

SITE ADDRESS:

USERNAME:

PASSWORD:

NOTE:

SITE NAME:

SITE ADDRESS:

USERNAME:

PASSWORD:

NOTE:

SITE NAME:

SITE ADDRESS:

USERNAME:

PASSWORD:

NOTE:

SITE NAME:

SITE ADDRESS:

USERNAME:

PASSWORD:

NOTE:

SITE NAME:

SITE ADDRESS:

USERNAME:

PASSWORD:

NOTE:

SITE NAME:

SITE ADDRESS:

USERNAME:

PASSWORD:

NOTE:

SITE NAME:

SITE ADDRESS:

USERNAME:

PASSWORD:

NOTE:

SITE NAME:

SITE ADDRESS:

USERNAME:

PASSWORD:

NOTE:

SITE NAME:

SITE ADDRESS:

USERNAME:

PASSWORD:

NOTE:

SITE NAME:

SITE ADDRESS:

USERNAME:

PASSWORD:

NOTE:

SITE NAME:

SITE ADDRESS:

USERNAME:

PASSWORD:

NOTE:

SITE NAME:

SITE ADDRESS:

USERNAME:

PASSWORD:

NOTE:

SITE NAME:

SITE ADDRESS:

USERNAME:

PASSWORD:

NOTE:

SITE NAME:

SITE ADDRESS:

USERNAME:

PASSWORD:

NOTE:

SITE NAME:

SITE ADDRESS:

USERNAME:

PASSWORD:

NOTE:

SITE NAME:

SITE ADDRESS:

USERNAME:

PASSWORD:

NOTE:

SITE NAME:

SITE ADDRESS:

USERNAME:

PASSWORD:

NOTE:

SITE NAME:

SITE ADDRESS:

USERNAME:

PASSWORD:

NOTE:

SITE NAME:

SITE ADDRESS:

USERNAME:

PASSWORD:

NOTE:

SITE NAME:

SITE ADDRESS:

USERNAME:

PASSWORD:

NOTE:

SITE NAME:

SITE ADDRESS:

USERNAME:

PASSWORD:

NOTE:

SITE NAME:

SITE ADDRESS:

USERNAME:

PASSWORD:

NOTE:

SITE NAME:

SITE ADDRESS:

USERNAME:

PASSWORD:

NOTE:

SITE NAME:

SITE ADDRESS:

USERNAME:

PASSWORD:

NOTE: